Published in 2018 by The Rosen Publishing Group, Inc.
29 East 21st Street, New York, NY 10010

Library of Congress Cataloging-in-Publication Data

Names: Vietze, Andrew, author.
Title: The life and death of Martin Luther King Jr. / Andrew Vietze.
Description: New York : Rosen Publishing, 2018 | Series:
Spotlight on the civil rights movement | Includes bibliographical references and index. | Audience: Grades 5–10.
Identifiers: LCCN 2017018779| ISBN 9781538380406 (library bound) | ISBN 9781538380390 (pbk.) | ISBN 9781538380383 (6 pack)
Subjects: LCSH: King, Martin Luther, Jr., 1929–1968—Juvenile literature. | African Americans—Biography—Juvenile literature. | Civil rights workers—United States—Biography—Juvenile literature. | African Americans—Civil rights—History—20th century—Juvenile literature. | Civil rights movements—United States—History—20th century—Juvenile literature.
Classification: LCC E185.97.K5 V54 2017 | DDC 323.092 [B]—dc23
LC record available at https://lccn.loc.gov/2017018779

Manufactured in China

On the cover: Martin Luther King Jr became the most recognizable face of the civil rights movement as he stood up to end the racial discrimination that had become entrenched in the American South after the Civil War.

CONTENTS

RIGHTS FOR ALL!

On February 18, 1957, *Time* magazine put a young black minister named Martin Luther King Jr. on its cover. It was a bold move. The country was in the midst of turmoil over race relations. Violence had broken out in the South against blacks, and people were marching in the streets, forming organizations and demanding an end to segregation, laws that kept blacks and whites separate—and unequal. As chairman of the Southern Christian Leadership Conference (SCLC), King became the most prominent black leader in the nation. Despite being stabbed, beaten, and unjustly arrested, he refused to give up on equality and justice, always advocating nonviolence. Thanks in part to his efforts, the country would see the official

A larger-than-life figure in his lifetime, Dr. Martin Luther King Jr. became one of the most famous individuals in American history.

end to policies of segregation. Martin Luther King Jr. would rise to become not just one of the most important voices in the fight for civil rights, but also one of the most important leaders in American history.

A KING IS BORN

Martin Luther King Jr. was born as Michael King Jr. on January 15, 1929, the second child of Alberta Williams King and Michael King. His father was a Baptist pastor who preached at the Ebenezer Baptist Church in Atlanta, and young Michael grew up in and around the church. His father formally changed his name to honor the founder of Protestantism, Martin Luther, in 1934. His son would follow in his footsteps. The Kings lived a comfortable, middle-class life. A bright and popular child, Martin Luther King Jr. cruised through school. When he was fourteen, he won a public-speaking contest. On the bus ride home, he was ordered to give up his seat when white passengers

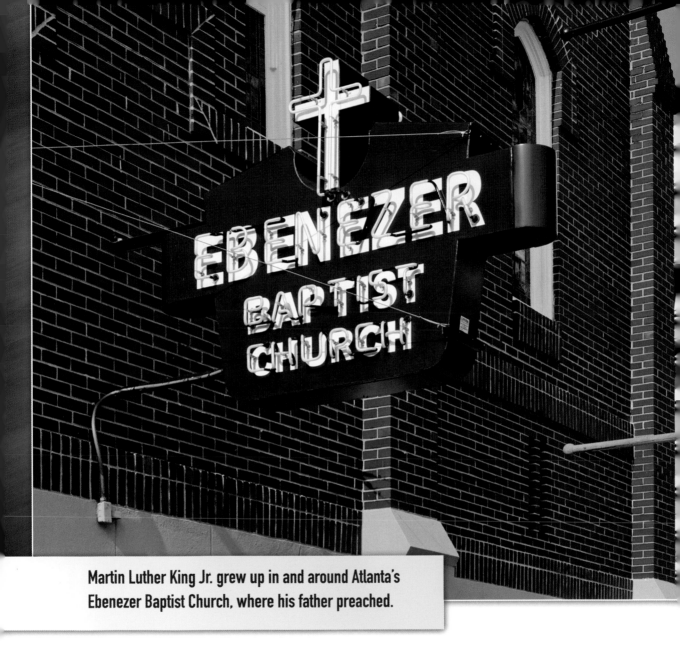

Martin Luther King Jr. grew up in and around Atlanta's Ebenezer Baptist Church, where his father preached.

boarded. He hesitated, and the bus driver swore at him. It was one of the first times he had come face-to-face with racial prejudice. King later said, "It was the angriest I have ever been in my life."

A PREACHER AND A DOCTOR

In his boyhood, Martin Luther King Jr. questioned religion. At thirteen, he expressed his doubt to his Sunday school teacher. He initially didn't want to follow the same path as his father, his uncle, and his grandfather to become a preacher. Instead, he enrolled at Morehouse College in Atlanta in 1944, at the age of fifteen, to study sociology. Before going to school, he took a job on a farm in Simsbury, Connecticut, and while he was there witnessed no racial prejudice. He was amazed a black man was allowed to eat anywhere a white man could. While in college, he took a Bible class and found his faith renewed. In 1948, he graduated with a degree in sociology and was ordained as a Baptist minister. He continued his education at Crozer Theological Seminary in Chester, Pennsylvania, graduating with a degree in divinity. He then attended Boston University, where he earned a doctorate in systematic theology in 1955.

The young Martin Luther King Jr. followed in his father's footsteps, becoming pastor of a Baptist church in Montgomery, Alabama.

LOVE AND MARRIAGE

In Boston, Martin Luther King Jr. met a young woman named Coretta Scott, from Alabama. Scott had graduated from Antioch College and now attended the New England Conservatory of Music, studying to be a concert singer. One of their first topics of conversation, on their very first date, was racial equality. Coretta Scott had feelings as strong as the young minister's. This pleased King, as he wanted a wife who shared his strong convictions and was an equal to him. After a brief courtship, Martin Luther King Jr. asked Coretta Scott to marry him. They were wed by Martin Luther King Sr. at her parents' home in Marion, Alabama, on June 18, 1953. A year later, the couple relocated to Montgomery, where Martin took a job at the Dexter Avenue Baptist Church. The move put him, without him even knowing it, right at the center of what was about to happen.

Dr. King's wife, Coretta Scott King, became an important civil rights leader in her own right.

MONTGOMERY EXPLODES

Racial tensions were heightened across the country—but especially in the South—over the Supreme Court's 1954 decision in *Brown v. Board of Education* that school segregation was unconstitutional. Whites across the South were offended that they would have to allow blacks into their classrooms. Things were about to get even more controversial. On December 1, 1955, a black woman named Rosa Parks refused to give up her seat to a white person while riding a bus in Montgomery, Alabama. King knew Parks from the Montgomery chapter of the National Association for the Advancement of Colored People (NAACP). She was the secretary of the organization, and he was on its executive committee. When she refused to make way for a white passenger,

Two of the most important figures in the push for civil rights in America, Dr. Martin Luther King Jr. and Rosa Parks, knew each other from the local chapter of the NAACP.

she was arrested. The Montgomery Improvement Association was put together to combat this injustice, and King was selected to lead the group.

BOYCOTT!

One of the Montgomery Improvement Association's first acts was a boycott of the Montgomery city bus system. "We have no alternative but to protest," said Martin Luther King Jr. after being elected president of the group. He told local blacks they shouldn't accept "anything less than freedom and justice." The Montgomery bus boycott made news across the country. It was difficult for all involved. Members of the black community had to find different ways to get to work and school, and they were harassed by whites as they walked on the street. The city, which operated the bus system, lost a lot of money. King and others filed a lawsuit claiming that segregation on buses shouldn't be legal, based on the Supreme Court's decision in the *Brown v. Board of Education* case. The highest court in the land had ruled, after all, that "separate is never equal."

The Montgomery bus boycott put the young reverend Martin Luther King Jr. on the American political map.

ATTACKS AND THREATS

Many southern whites were angry about the Supreme Court's decision that segregation was illegal and turned to violence. King's very public role in the boycott brought a lot of attention to him. At the end of January 1956, he received a threatening phone call. A few days later, his house was bombed. Luckily, no one was hurt. The attacks left King fearing for his life, until one morning, when he had an epiphany. He told an audience that he woke up and "rationality left me . . . almost out of nowhere I heard a voice that morning saying to me: 'Preach the Gospel, stand up for the truth, stand up for righteousness.'" After that moment, he lived without fear. He told his congregation: "Tell Montgomery they can keep shooting and I'm going to stand up to them; tell Montgomery they can keep bombing and I'm going to stand up to them."

Dr. King was a skilled and comfortable speaker to large audiences, thanks to his time preaching.

On November 13, 1956, the Supreme Court ruled that the Montgomery bus laws were unconstitutional. Martin Luther King Jr. was one of the first to ride on an integrated bus. The young leader was emboldened by the decision. He and other black ministers from the South founded the organization that became the Southern Christian Leadership Conference (SCLC) in 1957 to keep up the push for civil rights. Martin Luther King Jr. was named chairman. A month later, the twenty-eight-year-old minister was on the cover of *Time* as the face of the Montgomery bus boycott. In May, he gave his first national address, a speech called "Give Us the Ballot," at a rally of twenty-five thousand people at the Lincoln Memorial in Washington, DC. There, he implored the federal government to enforce antisegregation laws. And in June, King met with Vice President Richard Nixon to discuss civil rights. The Civil Rights Act of 1964 came about partially because of the events in Montgomery.

Dr. King spent a lot of time in courthouses fighting racially motivated charges against him. Here, a twenty-seven-year-old King emerges from the Montgomery Courthouse.

LEADING A NATION

Martin Luther King Jr.'s role with the SCLC made him more of a national figure than ever before. After the Washington, DC, event, he was considered, by the *New York Amsterdam News*, the country's "top Negro leader." In June 1958, King was part of a delegation of civil rights leaders that met with President Dwight D. Eisenhower. Later that year, his profile would rise even higher with the publication of his first book, *Stride Toward Freedom*. A memoir of the Montgomery bus affair, the book was a critical success and drew more attention to King's personal philosophies. In one chapter, King outlined his theories on nonviolence, which were inspired by the civil disobedience of Henry David Thoreau, the economic ideas of

Karl Marx, and the peaceful protests of Indian leader Mahatma Gandhi. King embarked on a tour to promote the book, and during a stop in Harlem, he was stabbed by a mentally unstable African American woman.

Dr. King forged important relationships with three presidents during his lifetime, including Dwight D. Eisenhower.

FIGHTING BY NOT FIGHTING

After the attack in Harlem, King was rushed to Harlem Hospital. He had a 7-inch (18-centimeter) letter opener embedded in his chest. It barely missed a major artery. King instantly forgave his attacker. After a brief recuperation, the young civil rights leader visited India upon the invitation of its leader, Jawaharlal Nehru. During the Montgomery boycott and in his book, King expressed his admiration of Mahatma Gandhi. So deep was his respect for the late Indian leader that he referred to his five-week trip to India as a "pilgrimage." The feelings were mutual—Indians, particularly the followers of Gandhi, had heard all about King. King and the Indians saw themselves as "brothers with the color of our skins," fighting a common enemy—racism.

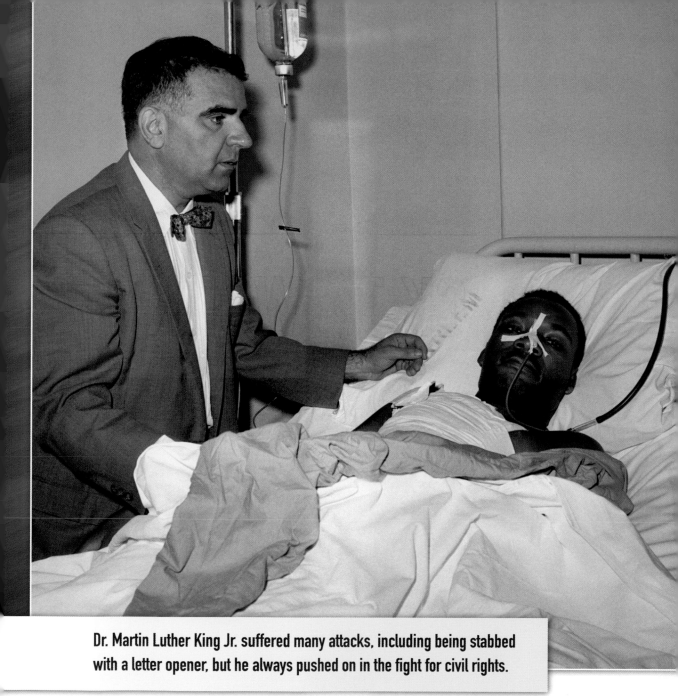

Dr. Martin Luther King Jr. suffered many attacks, including being stabbed with a letter opener, but he always pushed on in the fight for civil rights.

The man from Atlanta found the trip very inspirational and "was convinced more than ever before that the method of nonviolent resistance is the most potent weapon available to oppressed people."

BACK TO WORK

When King returned to the United States, he moved his family from Montgomery to Atlanta. He wanted to spend more time working on SCLC business. He took a job as assistant pastor, working with his father. And he continued to fight racism wherever he saw it. The SCLC began working closely with the Student Nonviolent Coordinating Committee (SNCC), a civil rights group made up mostly of college students. In October 1960, King and seventy-five students went to lunch at the lunch counter at one of Atlanta's prominent department stores. They sat at the counter, a space reserved for whites, and many, including Martin Luther King Jr., were arrested. Charges were dropped, but King was jailed on a matter related to a traffic violation. He was sentenced to four month's hard labor. President John F. Kennedy ordered him to be released.

Dr. King was arrested more than twenty-five times during his campaigns for civil rights. Here, he is escorted by police officers as he attends a hearing on a probation violation for assisting a student sit-in, which got him arrested.

FREEDOM RIDING

By 1961, many organizations were fighting for civil rights. Several black groups, like the Nation of Islam, led by Elijah Muhammad and Malcolm X, advocated that blacks take up arms to defend themselves. Roy Wilkins fought to end discrimination with the NAACP. Pacifist James Farmer urged the opposite, that blacks use peaceful methods to stand up for themselves. He asked people to support the Congress of Racial Equality (CORE) and organized bus trips to the South to make sure antisegregation laws were being followed. These trips, known as "Freedom Rides," were often attacked by racist whites. Students from many colleges in the North organized to see what they could do to help. Many boarded buses to take Freedom Rides to

The Freedom Riders put themselves at great risk to advocate for equal rights for all. Many were assaulted and hospitalized by racist southerners.

the South. In May 1961, Martin Luther King Jr. spoke during a visit by Freedom Riders at a Montgomery church. Soon, an angry mob gathered outside.

VIOLENCE IN MONTGOMERY

More than 1,500 people came to the church in Montgomery to welcome the Freedom Riders and hear speeches by Martin Luther King Jr. and other civil rights leaders.

An angry, violent crowd of more than 3,000 white racists besieged the church, and local and state police refused to intervene. The scene had been the same the day before when the bus that carried some of the Freedom Riders had arrived in the city.

Thugs armed with baseball bats, tire irons, and other weapons attacked the Freedom Riders while law enforcement officers stepped back and watched. Some people were badly wounded, and local hospitals refused to send ambulances to help.

At the church, US marshals were deployed to make sure no bombs were thrown but otherwise let the violent scene play out. The whites smashed windows, attacked blacks, and threw tear gas inside.

A bus transporting Freedom Riders was firebombed on May 14, 1961, by the Ku Klux Klan.

STANDING TALL

Dr. Martin Luther King Jr. stayed true to his word—he wouldn't back down in the face of violence. During the assault on the Montgomery church, he bravely walked outside through the mob. He continued the fight despite harsh treatment. Over the course of the next year, he was arrested multiple times for protesting. He once spoke about how he had a hard time explaining to his children why he was jailed so often. In September 1962, he was assaulted by a member of the American Nazi Party, who hit him repeatedly in the face. In 1963, he was arrested yet again in Birmingham, Alabama, and spent another week in lockup. During his time inside, he wrote a famous essay about nonviolence, the "Letter from a Birmingham Jail." Shortly after his release, Birmingham erupted with riots across the city after the bombing of the parsonage of Martin Luther King Jr.'s brother, Reverend A. D. King.

Dr. Martin Luther King Jr. is put in handcuffs and hauled away for "loitering" outside a courthouse.

MAN OF THE YEAR

On January 3, 1964, Martin Luther King Jr. was named Man of the Year by *Time* magazine. The magazine, one of the leading periodicals in the nation at the time, lauded King for his work on civil rights. He was the first African American ever to receive the honor. In December, he was invited to Oslo, Norway, to receive an even greater award—the Nobel Peace Prize—for his work toward racial equality. Typical of those turbulent times, during which people working for justice were jailed and harassed, and police stood by and watched the violent attacks, Martin Luther King Jr. was targeted by the Federal Bureau of Investigation (FBI) at the same time he was being celebrated. At the end of 1963, US attorney general Robert Kennedy authorized a wiretap at King's home. And the head of the FBI, the controversial J. Edgar Hoover, called King "the most notorious liar in the country."

Just thirty-five years old, Dr. Martin Luther King Jr. was the youngest person ever to receive the Nobel Peace Prize.

STRENGTH IN SELMA

Only 2 percent of blacks in the city of Selma, Alabama, were registered to vote. More than half of the population in the small city was African American, but they had almost no say in government. King, the SCLC, SNCC, and others organized Selma blacks to argue for voting rights. Because of the brutal local sheriff, their efforts had the potential to incite violence and draw national attention to the cause. Demonstrators were beaten by law enforcement. One protestor was shot and killed while trying to protect his mother from a police officer.

To protest the killing, organizers held a march from Selma to the state capital, Montgomery. The march ran into a blockade of law enforcement officers, who ordered the marchers to disperse.

Dr. Martin Luther King Jr. participated in a march in Selma, Alabama. After hundreds of protesters were attacked, and one killed, by the state police, the event became known as "Bloody Sunday."

When they refused, police savagely beat them. TV cameras captured the whole thing—to the outrage of the nation.

President Lyndon Johnson referred to the "outrage of Selma" upon signing the Voting Rights Act of 1965.

"I'VE BEEN TO THE MOUNTAINTOP"

Thanks to events like the Vietnam War, Martin Luther King Jr. began to see the American civil rights movement as part of a larger fight for social justice and equality happening around the globe. Civil rights and voting rights were crucial, but Dr. King realized that blacks would never get anywhere without economic security. In December 1967, he announced a plan for a Poor People's Campaign. Scheduled for May 1, 1968, the rally would be held at the nation's capital to demand jobs, a fair living wage, and economic justice. But first King would go to Memphis to march in solidarity with striking sanitation workers. While there, he delivered his famous "I've been to the mountaintop" speech. It would be the last speech he would ever make.

The old Lorraine Motel in Memphis, where Dr. Martin Luther King Jr. was shot and killed while talking on the balcony, is preserved as a historic site.

The next day, on April 4, 1968, Dr. Martin Luther King Jr. was shot by an assassin while standing on the balcony of his Memphis hotel.

LEGACY OF A KING

The sudden death of Martin Luther King Jr. stunned the nation. President Johnson declared April 7 a national day of mourning. Businesses, museums, and schools all closed, and the Academy Awards, baseball's opening day, and the NBA playoffs were postponed. Tributes poured in. King's funeral, held the next day at his boyhood church, was attended by many famous people and dignitaries, and more than one hundred thousand people paid tribute in the streets of Atlanta. Martin Luther King Jr. would go down as one of the great heroes of American history, bravely putting himself on the line for equality and justice, facing attacks, beatings, even death, with courage and honor.

Dr. Martin Luther King Jr. has been honored in many different ways since his assassination in 1968.

Without him, the Civil Rights Act of 1964 and the Voting Rights Act of 1965—huge strides toward equality for African Americans—would likely never have happened. In 1983, the US Congress voted to honor the legacy of the civil rights leader by making the third Monday of January a national holiday called Martin Luther King Jr. Day.

boycott To refuse to use or buy a company's goods or services.

civil disobedience Breaking the law as a means of protest.

congregation An audience gathered together, usually for religious reasons.

controversial Something that brings about disagreement.

convictions Strong beliefs.

coordinating Organizing or arranging.

delegation A group of people appointed to represent others.

discrimination Unfair treatment of groups of people, based on gender, race, religion, and the like.

dispersed Spread out or broken up.

embattled Involved in a battle.

epiphany A sudden idea, insight, or inspiration.

essay A written paper about an idea or theme.

executive The branch, group, or committee of an organization that puts laws into effect.

harassed Pressured, harried, and intimidated.

impassioned Full of passion.

impoverished Living in poverty.

notorious Famous, but not for good reasons.

parsonage The house where a minister lives.

prejudice A bias or opinion based on beliefs, not facts, like the racial hatred toward blacks.

procession A march or parade.

prominent Out front, important, placed where it can be seen.

Protestantism A branch of Christianity separate from the Catholic Church.

rationality Based on logic, thought, and reason.

segregation The act of keeping people separated.

solidarity Showing unity or support, especially for political reasons.

turmoil A state of unrest, uncertainty, and disturbance.

unconstitutional A law or act that goes against the word or spirit of the US Constitution.

wiretap A listening device that allows authorities to listen to conversations on a phone line.

Canadian Museum for Human Rights
85 Israel Asper Way
Winnipeg, MB R3C 0L5
Canada
(204) 289-2000
Website: https://humanrights.ca
Facebook: @canadianmuseumforhumanrights
Twitter: @CMHR_News
Instagram: @cmhr_mcdp
The museum showcases the human rights history of the United States'
    northerly neighbor.

The King Center
449 Auburn Avenue NE
Atlanta, GA 30312
(404) 526-8900
Website: http://www.thekingcenter.org
Facebook: @thekingcenter
Twitter: @TheKingCenter
The King Center is both a museum dedicated to the legacy of Martin Lu-
    ther King Jr. and a nonprofit organization pushing for social change.

Martin Luther King Jr. National Historic Site
450 Auburn Avenue NE
Atlanta, GA 30312
(404) 331-5190 x5046
Website: https://www.nps.gov/malu/index.htm
Facebook: @MartinLutherKingJr.NPS
Twitter: @MLKJr.NHSNPS

Instagram: @martinlutherkingJr.nps

The site is the most popular tourist destination in Atlanta. Facilities include the home where Martin Luther King Jr. was born, the church he attended, and places he played as a boy.

National Civil Rights Museum
450 Mulberry Street
Memphis, TN 38103
(901) 521-9699
Website: http://www.civilrightsmuseum.org
Facebook: @NCRMuseum
Twitter: @NCRMuseum
Instagram: @ncrmuseum

A museum located at the site where Martin Luther King Jr. was assassinated.

National Museum of African American History and Culture
1400 Constitution Avenue NW
Washington, DC 20560
(844) 750-3012
Website: https://nmaahc.si.edu
Facebook: @NMAAHC
Twitter: @nmaahc
Instagram: @nmaahc

Run by the Smithsonian Institution, this is the only national museum devoted to the African American experience.

WEBSITES

Because of the changing nature of internet links, Rosen Publishing has developed an online list of websites related to the subject of this book. This site is updated regularly. Please use this link to access this list:

http://www.rosenlinks.com/SCRM/MLK

Bader, Bonnie, and Nancy Harrison. *Who Was Martin Luther King?* New York, NY: Grosset and Dunlap, 2007.

Clayton, Ed. *Martin Luther King: The Peaceful Warrior.* New York, NY: Simon Pulse, 2001.

Flowers, Arthur, and Manu Chitrakar. *I See the Promised Land: A Life of Martin Luther King Jr.* Toronto, ON, Canada: Groundwood Books, 2013.

Jeffrey, Gary, and Chris Forsey. *Martin Luther King, Jr.: The Life of a Civil Rights Leader.* New York, NY: Rosen Publishing, 2006.

King, Dr. Martin Luther, Jr. *I Have a Dream/Letter from Birmingham Jail.* Logan, IA: Perfection Learning, 1990.

King, Dr. Martin Luther, Jr. *I Have a Dream: Writings and Speeches That Changed the World.* St. Louis, MO: Turtleback Books, 2003.

King, Dr. Martin Luther, Jr. *A Time to Break the Silence: The Essential Works of Dr. Martin Luther King Jr. for Students.* Boston, MA: Beacon Press, 2013.

Schuman, Michael A. *The Life of Martin Luther King Jr.* New York, NY: Enslow Publishing, 2014.

Teitelbaum, Michael, and Lewis Helfand. *Martin Luther King, Jr.: Let Freedom Ring.* New Delhi, India: Campfire, 2013.

Walker, Ida. *The Assassination of Dr. Martin Luther King Jr.* Minneapolis, MN: ABDO Publishing, 2008.

International Civil Rights Center and Museum. "America's Civil Rights Timeline." https://www.sitinmovement.org/history/america-civil-rights-timeline.asp.

King, Dr. Martin Luther, Jr. "Martin Luther King's I Have a Dream Speech, August 28, 1963." American History: From Revolution to Reconstruction and Beyond. http://www.let.rug.nl/usa/documents/1951-/martin-luther-kings-i-have-a-dream-speech-august-28-1963.php.

King, Dr. Martin Luther, Jr., and Clayborn Carson. *The Autobiography of Martin Luther King Jr.* New York, NY: Warner Books, 2001.

King, Dr. Martin Luther, Jr., and James M. Washington. *A Testament of Hope: The Essential Writings and Speeches of Martin Luther King Jr.* San Francisco, CA: HarperOne, 2003.

Library of Congress. "Martin Luther King Jr." America's Story: From America's Library. http://www.americaslibrary.gov/aa/king/aa_king_subj.html.

Stanford University, The Martin Luther King Jr. Research and Education Institute. "Major King Events Chronology 1929–1968." https://kinginstitute.stanford.edu/king-resources/major-king-events-chronology-1929-1968.

ABOUT THE AUTHOR

Andrew Vietze is the best-selling author of several biographies of great Americans, including Rosen's Spotlight on the Civil Rights Movement title, *The Life and Death of Malcolm X*. His work has been featured on the Travel Channel and has won multiple awards. Martin Luther King Jr. is one of his heroes. Find out more at www.andrewvietze.com.

PHOTO CREDITS

Designer: Nelson Sá; Editor and Photo Researcher: Xina M. Uhl